Neuschwanstein Castle

by Grace Hansen

Abdo
FAMOUS CASTLES
Kids

Abdo Kids Jumbo is an Imprint of Abdo Kids
abdobooks.com

abdobooks.com

Published by Abdo Kids, a division of ABDO, P.O. Box 398166, Minneapolis, Minnesota 55439.
Copyright © 2022 by Abdo Consulting Group, Inc. International copyrights reserved in all countries.
No part of this book may be reproduced in any form without written permission from the publisher.
Abdo Kids Jumbo™ is a trademark and logo of Abdo Kids.

Printed in the United States of America, North Mankato, Minnesota.

052021

092021

THIS BOOK CONTAINS
RECYCLED MATERIALS

Photo Credits: Alamy, Granger Collection, iStock, Shutterstock

Production Contributors: Teddy Borth, Jennie Forsberg, Grace Hansen
Design Contributors: Candice Keimig, Pakou Moua

Library of Congress Control Number: 2020947653
Publisher's Cataloging-in-Publication Data

Names: Hansen, Grace, author.

Title: Neuschwanstein castle / by Grace Hansen

Description: Minneapolis, Minnesota : Abdo Kids, 2022 | Series: Famous castles | Includes online resources
    and index.

Identifiers: ISBN 9781098207311 (lib. bdg.) | ISBN 9781098208158 (ebook) | ISBN 9781098208578
    (Read-to-Me ebook)

Subjects: LCSH: Schloss Neuschwanstein (Germany)--Juvenile literature. | Castles--Juvenile literature. |
    Architecture--Juvenile literature.

Classification: DDC 728.81--dc23

Table of Contents

The Fairytale Castle

Up in the Bavarian Alps lies a castle fit for a fairy tale. Unlike many castles, Neuschwanstein never had a military purpose. Built by the shy King Ludwig II, it was meant for privacy.

King Ludwig II

Germany

Europe

Neuschwanstein
Castle

Work on the castle's site began in 1868. First, the ruins of two smaller castles were removed. Stone also had to be cleared. Then, the **foundation** was laid.

project drawing

The main *Palas* began taking form in 1872. The two-story Throne Room was part of the *Palas*. Beautiful paintings and decorations cover its walls.

9

The castle was built with **modern** technology in mind. It had electric bell and lift systems. The castle also had running water on each floor.

The first building to be completed was the Gateway Building in 1873. Ludwig II could stay there and oversee the project.

Gateway Building

13

The King's Death

On June 13, 1886, Ludwig II's body was found in a lake. His death was very mysterious. To this day, no one is sure what happened to him.

LUDWIG II.
KÖNIG v. BAYERN.

1886   1906.

geb. 25. Aug. 1845   gest. 13. Juni 188

LUDWIG II.·KÖNIG VON BAYERN

15

The king had big and expensive plans for the castle. Only about 14 rooms in the castle were finished when he died. The remaining plans were simplified or thrown out.

17

The castle was opened to the public just weeks after the king's death. The castle and its grounds are beautiful.

The Castle Today

Meant for just one man, today the castle accepts many guests. More than 1 million people visit Neuschwanstein each year. Its charm attracts people from all around the world.

More Facts

- The foundation for the castle was laid on September 5, 1869. In it, portraits of Ludwig II and coins with his face were placed. This was a tradition started by the king's grandfather, Ludwig I.

- Ludwig II's childhood summer home was originally called *Schwanstein*. It was built on a stone (*stein*) overlooking lake Schwansee (*schwan* meaning "swan"). The word *Neu* or "New" was added to name the castle.

- Disneyland's Sleeping Beauty Castle was inspired by Neuschwanstein. Walt Disney and his wife visited the castle while on a tour of Europe.

Glossary

Bavarian Alps – range of the Alps between Bavaria, Germany and Tyrol, Austria.

foundation – a strong structure that holds up a building from beneath.

modern – of or having to do with the latest ideas.

palas – a German term for the imposing or large building of a castle that contained the great hall.

privacy – the condition of being alone or away from the view of other people.

Index

Abdo Kids ONLINE
FREE! ONLINE MULTIMEDIA RESOURCES

Visit **abdokids.com**

to access crafts, games, videos, and more!

Use Abdo Kids code

FNK7311

or scan this QR code!